# RAIN FORESTS & REEFS

## A KID'S-EYE VIEW OF THE TROPICS

Written by Caitlin Maynard and Thane Maynard
Photographs by Stan Rullman

FRANKLIN WATTS    A DIVISION OF GROLIER PUBLISHING
NEW YORK    LONDON    HONG KONG    SYDNEY    DANBURY, CONNECTICUT

## THE TEAM

Caitlin Maynard is a fourteen-year-old middle school student who shares her journal of the trip and her experiences in the tropics. Stan Rullman, leader of the Junior Zoologists Club, took the pictures that document this adventure. Thane Maynard, director of education at the zoo, added the facts and figures.

*The Junior Zoologists Club*

Maps by Cincinnati Zoo (Joanna Wright)
Photographs copyright © Cincinnati Zoo (Stan Rullman)
Library of Congress Cataloging-in-Publication Data
Maynard, Caitlin.
    Rain forests and reefs : a kid's-eye view of the tropics / by Caitlin Maynard, Thane Maynard, and Stan Rullman.
        p.    cm.
    Includes bibliographical references (p.  ) and index.
    Summary: Describes a fieldtrip that eighteen students and seven adults took to study the ecosystems of a tropical rain forest and a coral reef in Belize.
    ISBN 0-531-11281-0 (lib. bdg.)    ISBN 0-516-15806-3 (pbk.)
    1. Rain forest ecology—Belize—Juvenile literature.  2. Coral reef ecology—Belize—Juvenile literature.  3. Rain forests—Belize—Juvenile literature.  4. Coral reefs and islands—Belize—Juvenile literature. [1. Rain forest ecology—Belize. 2. Rain forests—Belize. 3. Coral reef ecology—Belize. 4. Coral reefs and islands—Belize. 5. Ecology—Belize.] I. Maynard, Thane. II. Rullman, Stan. III. Title.
QH108.B43M39    1996
574.5'2642'097282—dc20
                                                    96-33974
                                                    CIP
                                                    AC

MEXICO

UNITED STATES

Rain Forests and Reefs *is dedicated to Stan Rullman, who has lead a generation of young naturalists on adventures afield, and always made sure that they brought along their sense of wonder.*

C. M. & T. M.

CUBA

BELIZE

Cockscomb Basin
Jaguar Preserve

← Belize Barrier Reef

★ ← Ranguana Cay

CENTRAL
AMERICA

SOUTH AMERICA

## WHAT THIS BOOK IS ABOUT

*It appears to me that nothing can be more improving to a young naturalist than a journey in distant countries.*

CHARLES DARWIN
*1845*

In June of 1994, eighteen teenage students, six adults, and I, the group leader, journeyed to the Central American country of Belize. The students were members of the Cincinnati Zoo's Junior Zoologists Club, a club started in 1968 to help interested students take the first step on the path to becoming biologists. Each group of teenagers meets at the zoo for weekly classes and heads out into "the field" to explore areas of natural history in the Midwest. Every summer we embark on a field study in an ecosystem different from our own backyards. We've studied such habitats as the Greater Yellowstone Ecosystem, the lakes and streams of the northern woods in Algonquin Provincial Park in Ontario, Canada, the frigid waters off the rocky coast of Maine, and also the neotropical rain forests of Costa Rica, Guatemala, Trinidad, and Belize.

However, this book is not a travelogue, nor a look at some lucky teenagers "on a holiday," nor a "what I did on my summer vacation" report. It *is* an introduction to the two most life-filled, diverse habitats on Earth—the tropical rain forests and the coral reefs—as seen through the eyes of a kid, one of the participants, with some background commentary and photographs by two of the adults lucky enough to go along. It is also a book that considers the threatened disappearance of these habitats and some possible solutions to their problems. So, put on your insect repellent, grab your shades, and eat a good breakfast. The only R&R on this summer trip are the *rain forests & reefs.*

STAN RULLMAN
*Cincinnati Zoo and Botanical Garden*

Dear Ms. Greenbaum,

This is even better than I expected!
The sounds, sights, and even the people seem exotic!
I'm really excited about the days ahead. I'm glad we studied the rain forest in school. Now I can see it with my own eyes.

Caitlin Maynard

Ms. Greenbaum
17 School Street
Cincinnati, Ohio
45215
U.S.A.

## How Could A Place So Hot And Humid Be So Cool?

It's easier and faster to get to the rain forest and coral reefs of Central America than it is to fly across the United States. We—the Junior Zoologists and company—arrived in Belize City, the former capital of Belize and the only place in Belize with a big airport, after a four-hour flight from Cincinnati, Ohio. A few years ago a hurricane hit the coastal capital and left it in ruins. So a new capital, Belmopan, was built inland, in the highlands. The airport is still on the coast because many tourists come to Belize to visit coral reefs and to fish and snorkel.

The rain forest—our first morning view

We worked hard on this trip. In the rain forest we hiked through hot, wet air for four-teen miles on some days, and up to another five miles at night.

It was an exhausting but really exciting trip. We had many terrific experiences. We saw hundreds of species of birds, mammals, plants, and insects, more than I would ever see in a forest in North America. I saw things that I had only read about, or seen on television.

The coral reef was as exciting as the forest. The color of the water, the fish, the coral—there was so much to look at. I was in a whole new underwater world. We also camped on a deserted island. I have never seen so many stars in a night sky!

I will never forget this experience. It started in a small Central American city on a June night, when the air was more hot and humid than on any summer day in my hometown. The night air was filled with the sounds of insects. One I would even take home with me!

We arrived in Belize City in the evening and headed off for the rain forest right away. As we drove to our first camp, it grew darker and darker. By the time we reached our cabins, a full moon had risen. We piled out of our battered bus and looked upon a forest lit by moonlight. Just where were we? We spent the next two weeks exploring this magical world.

Journal writing

## LEARNING TO LOOK

Our first hike in the rain forest was a little weird. We had been studying tropical **biodiversity** for months and knew the facts and figures. There are more animals here than anywhere. In fact, if you weighed them, rain forest creatures from one site would outweigh even the large mammals of Africa from an area the same size. So, I wondered, where are they all hiding?

The problem was mostly green. In a **rain forest** that's all you see at first, green leaves everywhere. You could say that you can't see the critters for the trees, but after a while we learned to look and listen for the movement, color, and diversity all around.

*All around us, everything was green.*

6

Our studies began right away and did not end until we were back on the plane two weeks later.

We found leaf-cutter-ant trails cutting across our path every day, with thousands of ants running back and forth, carrying pieces of leaves back to their underground "cities." That's the equivalent of humans sprinting thirty miles with grand pianos in their mouths! The ants chew up the leaves in order to grow a special **fungus**, which they then eat. The ants and the fungus are interdependent—each depends on the other. This fungal species has not been found growing outside of the ant colonies.

We also saw army ants that live in traveling colonies of as many as a million ants. These ants form huge raiding columns and travel in search of prey. They feed on small animals, even baby birds and lizards. These ants and the antbird form another interdependent relationship. The antbirds follow the army ants, depending on their advance to scatter the insects on the forest floor. The birds feed on the ants' leftovers! And certain butterflies feed on the antbird's droppings.

*A column of army ants on the march*

There are many other interdependent plants and animals in this region, because rainforest species need as much help as they can get to survive!

# Don Murray

*Don Murray grew up rock climbing on the craggy moun- tains of Scotland, but now he climbs around in the trees of the hot, humid tropical forest. He is a botanist who studies epiphytes, plants that live on other "host" plants and get nutrients from the air and rain, instead of from the soil.*

Don is researching interrelationships between the animals and plants of the forest canopy. Each morning before sunrise, he hikes two miles through the forest to his study site. The plants he is studying are generally found between 60 and 120 feet up in the trees, so instead of struggling up the tree trunks each day—trunks covered with sharp thorns and biting ants—Don ascends by a network of straps and harnesses and a device called a Jumar ascender. Mountain climbers developed this system, which is now used to climb hundreds of feet into the forest canopy. This system allows scientists to study an area for long periods of time without much disturbance.

*Don Murray describes his research on the relation-ships between epiphytes (plants that grow on other plants) and the animals of the rain forest and shows how the ascender helps him get to his study site in the forest canopy.*

*A bromeliad*

In a single tropical forest tree, Don has found that as many as 64 species of animals interact with a three-inch-tall bromeliad, one of his study plants. Some drink water from the plant's central cup, some lay eggs on its leaves, or use it for food or shelter. As many as two thousand species of animals and plants can live on and in a single mature rain forest tree. Now that's a wildlife apartment house.

# TROPICAL TERMINOLOGY

## SYMBIOSIS

*A predator—the spider—waiting for its prey.*

Sometimes people think that symbiosis and cooperation are the same, but symbiosis really refers to an interrelationship between two living creatures. Sometimes both parties benefit, as when a clown fish cleans an anemone. A predator-prey relationship is another form of symbiosis. Ecologists describe three categories of symbiosis.

In MUTUALISM, both organisms benefit in a win-win situation. A good mutualism example is pollination. Birds, insects, and bats help plants reproduce by transporting their pollen; the transporters get a nectar meal as payment.

In COMMENSALISM, one party benefits without much effect on the other. The epiphytes, or air plants, that live on the branches of rain forest trees need big trees to live on, but have no effect on the host tree.

In PARISITISM, one animal or plant benefits to the detriment of another species. The tropics are full of parasites. Many, such as the tachinid flies, are so small they live inside other creatures. Others, like strangler figs, can be as tall as a tree, but as they grow they can eventually kill their host.

Remember, symbiosis is essential. The species cannot live without their relationship with each other.

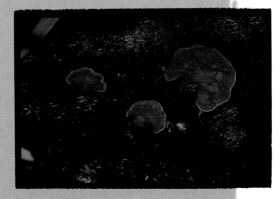

*Fungi at the base of a tree. The fungi extract nutrients from the soil and exchange them for nutrients from the trees. This exchange takes place between the trees' rootlets and the fungi. Each species cannot live without its relationship with the other species.*

Dear Mom,
We have seen so many different species of birds on this trip, including the keel-billed toucan. I saw more than five species of songbirds on a single bush! Everything in Belize is so much more diverse than in the United States. love, Cai—

Kathleen Maynard
20 Main Street
Cincinnati, Ohio
45215

*A congregation of bird species: a pair of red-legged honeycreepers, a white collared seed-eater, an oriole, and a scarlet-rumped tanager share a shrub.*

### BIOFACTS

**BELIZE IS A COUNTRY ABOUT THE SIZE OF MASSACHUSETTS, YET IT IS HOME TO MORE THAN 500 BIRD SPECIES.**

By comparison, there are only 800 bird species in all of Canada and the United States.

The keel-billed toucan is the bird most people picture as a "toucan." This black bird, with a yellow chest and face, and a huge, brightly colored bill, is the largest species of toucan. It is sometimes called the banana-bill toucan, but in Belize most of the people simply called it the "bill-bird." Another toucan species we saw is the beautiful collared aracari. This smaller toucan is black with a yellow and red chest, a red rump, and

An aracari

a white and black bill. The only other toucan in Belize is the emerald toucanet. Its bright green color allows it to blend into the rain forest, so it is very difficult to find.

There are 319 species of hummingbirds in the world. There are about forty species in Belize; we saw fewer than ten. It is a challenge to find these

*Hummingbirds: a green–crowned brilliant (female), and a violet sabrewing.*

tiny birds, because of their amazing adaptations. They are very active, and can fly at incredibly fast speeds—forward or backward—and can also hover. They beat their wings up to eighty times a second. Because of all this activity they are in constant need of food. They fly from flower to flower drinking up the nectar to power their small but mighty bodies. They often carry tiny mites on their bills, which are transported to different flowers. We searched the flowers and leaves of the forests, looking for these spectacular flyers.

The hummingbirds play an important role in the life cycle of the forest. Flying from flower to flower, they cross-pollinate as they feed. This means healthier plants, more flowers, and more nectar for the "hummers."

## Flowers and Pollination

Most flowers in the rain forest depend on insects, birds, and bats to pollinate them. Wind pollination is practically impossible in the rain forest because the plant life is so dense, except where emergent trees grow out of the top of the canopy. Vertebrates, like bats and hummingbirds, and thousands of invertebrates, mostly insects, carry out pollination here.

While hiking, we saw dozens of species of flowers, including amazing orchids. They were brightly colored, with unique scents. Some you could eat!

Flowers that are pollinated by hummingbirds usually have long tubes. They are most often red, orange, or yellow. Bat-pollinated flowers open at night, and usually have a musky scent that attracts bats. The flowers are white, which enables bats to find them at night. Most rain forest flowers can be pollinated by several species, although some rely on one species to transfer their pollen.

*A tropical orchid*

*A heliconia*

14

# TROPICAL **TERMINOLOGY**

## WHAT'S THE BIG DEAL ABOUT BIODIVERSITY?

"Bio" means life and "diversity" means variety, so biodiversity is the great variety of all life on Earth. All forms of life—from tiny bacteria to giant whales—play important roles in how nature works. The trouble is many species are becoming extinct, or disappearing forever, before we even know about them.

Rain forests and coral reefs display the greatest biodiversity of any habitats on Earth.

Biodiversity not only means lots of different species, but also the diversity of ecosystems and genetic varieties within each species. Nature works like a big, complicated, and interconnected system, so protecting biodiversity is vital for living species—human and wild.

There is an amazing diversity of hawks, falcons, and vultures in Belize. We saw many as we hiked high into the mountain regions. Almost every time we climbed into the buses to head out to another study site, we saw a road-side hawk, with beautiful gray-brown feathers. We also saw the bat falcon—a black-backed bird with white and orange patches. This small falcon hunts at sunrise and sunset because its main prey is bats. It is so fast, it catches bats in flight. We also saw laughing falcons, named for their loud call that pierces through the forest.

We saw a number of different species of vultures in Belize. These are nature's recyclers and in the forest they have lots of work. Besides the black vultures and turkey vultures that we have at home, we also saw magnificent king vultures with brightly colored heads. During one hike, seven vultures were soaring in a "kettle" above our heads. Most were king vultures.

*A king vulture*

Dear Alison,

Today we went to the 1000-foot falls. The waterfall is even higher than Niagara Falls! There were lots of hawks and falcons. We were above the birds, instead of the birds being above us! See you soon! Caitlin

Alison Freeman
75 Highland Circle
Cincinnati, Ohio
45215
U.S.A.

LPC 10

16

# Mountain Pine Ridge

Not all tropical forests are the same. We saw this when we visited the 1,000-Foot Falls along a stream that cuts a valley through the Mountain Pine Ridge region of Belize. This forest reminded us of the Smokey Mountains with its terrain and predominant pine trees. The change in elevation, the topsoil, and the humidity make this forest very different from the broadleaf lowland forests in other areas.

*The 1,000-Foot Falls. Actually, the distance from top to bottom is 1,700 feet, and the waterfall ranks as the seventh highest in the world.*

## BIOFACTS

**OVER ONE-FOURTH OF ALL PRESCRIPTION DRUGS SOLD TODAY WERE ORIGINALLY DERIVED FROM PLANTS.**

As yet, less than 5 percent of all plants have even been studied for their medicinal value.

# Osta Von Unger

Osta Von Unger is a German teenager who came to Central America to start an environmental education program at the Slate Creek Reserve in central Belize. She works with local schools to get young Belizeans out in the forest, and to help them learn about both natural history and the cultural heritage of the Mayan people.

Osta and the staff at Mountain Equestrian Trails, a tent camp inside the reserve, are teaching people about the rain forest through experiential learning. By hiking the trails and camping in the forest, young Belizeans come to love the nature around them. Osta also takes slides and cultural artifacts to schools in the region to show groups there the importance of protecting Belize's remaining wild areas.

*Osta Von Unger explains why saving the rain forests of Central America is important to her, and to us.*

## RAIN FOREST REMEDIES

For thousands of years the Mayan people have lived in the mountains and forests of Mexico and Central America. Like native peoples around the world, over the centuries they developed traditional medicines from local plants to treat many kinds of ailments. These medicines are being studied by **ethnobotanists** and drug companies looking for new drugs from the ancient Mayan traditions.

WILD YAM—Traditionally used in a variety of remedies. Derivatives have been used in a number of modern medicines.

CACAO—Perhaps the most popular rain forest plant in the world, the cacao pod is the source of chocolate. Chocolate is not technically a medicine, but sometimes it is good for what ails you. And it does contain caffeine, which is a stimulant.

BAY CEDAR—These leaves are boiled to make a tea to treat dysentery and diarrhea.

ALLSPICE—Berries and leaves are brewed to treat digestive problems and are ground into a paste for the treatment of athlete's foot.

GIVE-AND-TAKE—This tree's name comes from its double role: it gives a painful, stinging cut which can then be remedied by rubbing the leaves on the cut to stop the bleeding.

DOG'S TONGUE—The leaves of this tree are used in an herbal bath that helps to cure insomnia.

*The fruit of the cacao plant, from which we get chocolate, grows right on the trunk.*

# Rosita Arvigo

Dr. Rosita Arvigo welcomes visitors to the Panti Medicine Trail.

Outside of Belize, ethnobotanist Dr. Rosita Arvigo is well known as the author of the books *Rain Forest Remedies: 100 Healing Herbs of Belize* and *Sastun: My Apprenticeship with a Maya Healer.* She has taken part in dozens of medical conferences, always eager to share her knowledge of traditional medical practices.

Within the country of Belize, however, Rosita is more of a legend. Each year thousands of people visit the medicinal trail she created in the eastern highlands. Rosita and her staff take visitors on guided tours, showing them the native plants growing there and how they are used. Many of the visitors are Belizeans coming to purchase natural cures. Others are tourists drawn by the stories they have heard about this "medicine woman." And many more are doctors and researchers from hospitals, universities, and pharmaceutical companies around the world, all hoping to learn about the bounty and mystery of the forest.

*A guide leads visitors on a tour of the medicine trail.*

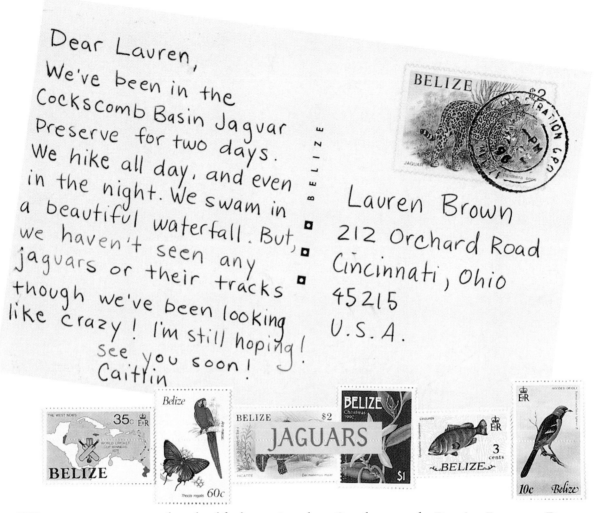

Dear Lauren,
We've been in the Cockscomb Basin Jaguar Preserve for two days. We hike all day, and even in the night. We swam in a beautiful waterfall. But, we haven't seen any jaguars or their tracks though we've been looking like crazy! I'm still hoping! See you soon!
Caitlin

Lauren Brown
212 Orchard Road
Cincinnati, Ohio
45215
U.S.A.

We spent two and a half days in the Cockscomb Basin Jaguar Preserve hiking, studying, and looking for these huge, spotted cats. Jaguars were what the group most wanted to see.

The Cockscomb Basin Jaguar Preserve is the first area set aside for the conservation of wild cats. For jaguars to survive, they need a place to live—and for jaguars, that place has to be large! The preserve consists of 102,000 acres. One day we hiked for hours, but when we got back and looked at the map, we saw that we had covered only a tiny portion of the preserve. And this huge piece of land is home for only about twenty-five jaguars! Each cat needs at least four thousand acres for hunting and living. That is why fewer and fewer jaguars can be found in the world. The growing human population is crowding out the animals.

*The only jaguars we saw were at the Belize Zoo.*

*Project Jaguar—the sanctuary in the preserve*

The jaguar is a large, six-foot-long cat that people often confuse with the smaller leopard. It weighs up to 350 pounds. This huge cat has no predators except for, occasionally, the gigantic anaconda of the Amazon and, of course, humans. Jaguars are "generalists," meaning they live in all types of forests, **savannas,** and even **mangroves.** They feed on many kinds of animals: deer, fish, birds, and reptiles. They attack with a mighty leap and a great big bite. They are very solitary and nocturnal.

Although we did not find a jaguar, we did explore their **habitat.** We could feel their presence. And, while we didn't see one of them in the wild, I bet one of them saw us!

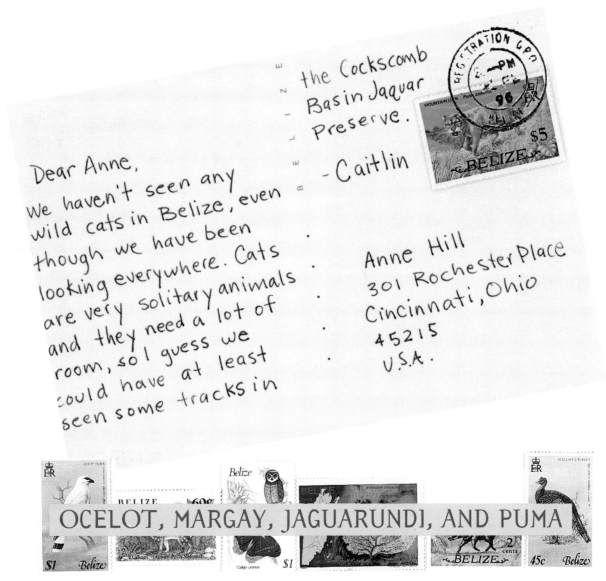

Dear Anne,
We haven't seen any wild cats in Belize, even though we have been looking everywhere. Cats are very solitary animals and they need a lot of room, so I guess we could have at least seen some tracks in the Cockscomb Basin Jaguar Preserve.

— Caitlin

Anne Hill
301 Rochester Place
Cincinnati, Ohio
45215
U.S.A.

## OCELOT, MARGAY, JAGUARUNDI, AND PUMA

Ocelots are among the most beautiful cats in the world, famous for their spotted fur. Unfortunately, this is one reason that ocelots are endangered. A good rule to remember is that *furs look better on their original owners.*

The margay is sometimes mistaken for its larger cousin the ocelot. They are very similar in color and markings, but the margay, being smaller, tends to eat smaller prey. Margays live up in the canopy and understory of rain forest trees and hunt at night for small mammals.

The jaguarundi is the least known of the cats. It is a long-legged cat with a solid brown coat that dwells in lowland forests and swamps. Like nearly all cats, jaguarundis are nocturnal.

The puma is one of the most wide-ranging animals in the world. At one time this species lived throughout all of North, Central, and South America. As a result, it has many names: Florida panther, cougar, screamer, and catamount, plus other names in local languages.

*A puma*

## Cockscomb Basin Jaguar Preserve

We have been at C.B.J.P. for two days. On our first night we took a night hike into the forest. We saw the "eyeshine" of a kinkajou. And, unluckily, we took a trail also traveled by a colony of red ants! This was our first look at this giant preserve. We went to sleep hot and woke up to the heat and humidity of a June day in the basin. We hiked to a really wonderful part of the forest, an area of huge, tall trees with enormous buttress roots. The sunlight filtered down to the leaf-carpeted floor, and a breeze even cooled us off a little. The vines hanging down were covered with fungi, bromeliads, orchids, and other exotic plants. Each of us chose a tree and leaned back in the curve of its roots.

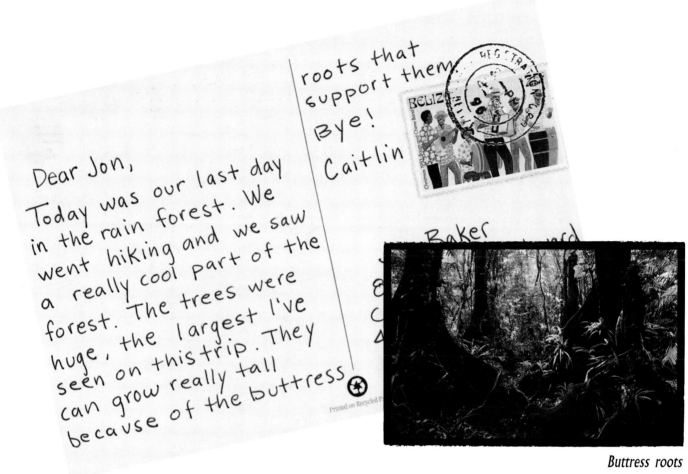

Dear Jon,
Today was our last day in the rain forest. We went hiking and we saw a really cool part of the forest. The trees were huge, the largest I've seen on this trip. They can grow really tall because of the buttress roots that support them.
Bye!
Caitlin

Buttress roots

BUTTRESS ROOTS

Buttress roots are huge, flange-like root systems that support trees in the rain forest. These roots flare out at the bottom of the tree, the way a tripod spreads out to steady the spotting scope we use to watch wildlife. In the rain forest there is very little topsoil, usually only a couple of inches, as compared with the nearly two feet of topsoil in temperate forests. The buttress roots support the tree over a large area since the tree's roots cannot grow deep into the ground for support.

25

# Waterfalls, Monkeys, and a Tree Frog

When we got back to base camp for lunch we were incredibly hot and thirsty and ready for a break. We convinced our leader to hike to a waterfall! After a morning of heat and humidity it was great to jump into a stream with a deep pool created by a waterfall!

*Cooling off, Belize style*

That evening Linde Ostro and Scott Silver came to tell us about another species of mammal living in the preserve. They were studying two different groups of howler monkeys that were translocated to this part of the forest by scientists. These researchers had been searching all day for one of the groups and hadn't been able to locate them.

Later we went on another night hike. Our guide, Nathan, took us down a dirt road. He caught a roosting paraque, a member of

*Our guide catches a paraque. These nocturnal birds feed on night-flying insects.*

the nightjar family, BY HAND! Nathan walked slowly, slowly, up to the bird while shining his flashlight in its eyes. Then, like lightning, he grabbed it! We all looked by flashlight and then we let it go. We also found a red-eyed tree frog right in the road. What luck! This symbol of the rain forest was just sitting there for us to see.

At the end of the hike we all lay down in the road and looked up at the sky. There were stars everywhere, with no competing lights to block their shine. I realized I was looking at the sky from a whole different place on Earth. Stan asked us to think about our feelings about the forest. But mostly we were silent. I couldn't help wondering about the jaguar! It was entirely possible that one was looking at us at that very moment, because we were in the rain forest, where everything was aware of us but we were just learning to be aware of our surroundings.

Early the next morning we went for our last hike in this beautiful forest. As we wandered we found the missing group of howler monkeys! This was the most exciting wild mammal we saw in Belize. We stood under the branches and watched these smaller primates gracefully travel through the trees.

*A red-eyed tree frog*

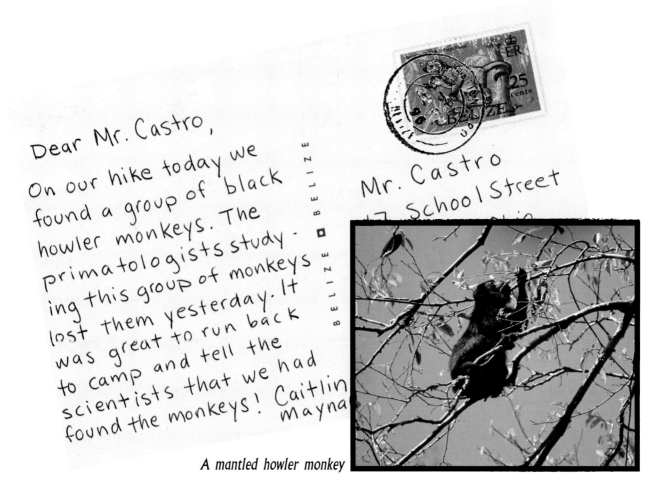

Dear Mr. Castro,

On our hike today we found a group of black howler monkeys. The primatologists studying this group of monkeys lost them yesterday. It was great to run back to camp and tell the scientists that we had found the monkeys! Caitlin Mayna

Mr. Castro
17 School Street

A mantled howler monkey

## HOWLER MONKEYS: ARBOREAL MEANS IT'S COOL TO HANG IN TREES

Howler monkeys are the best-known monkeys in the **Neotropics.** Their loud, ferocious calls can be heard throughout the forest. There are many species of howlers, each named for its color. Different troops define their territory by their calls and never even see each other. Male howlers are dominant and bigger than the females. An average family group has three males, seven or eight females, and any number of juveniles. A clan can have four to thirty-five monkeys. The monkeys eat leaves, flowers, and fruit. They live high up in the trees, and are more often heard than seen.

We saw the best wildlife after dark. Kinkajous and olingos, for instance, are small animals with tan to brown coats. They are nocturnal and hunt in the tree branches during the night. They resemble monkeys with their front-facing eyes and prehensile, or grasping, tails. Both are actually members of the prosionid family and are related to raccoons. They are omnivorous, feeding on fruits, insects, and smaller mammals.

*The olingo, a relative of the kinkajou and the raccoon, is usually nocturnal, although it sometimes comes out in daylight to raid a hummingbird feeder.*

## TROPICAL PROFILES

# Linde Ostro and Scott Silver

Many field studies of tropical plant and animal species are conducted by graduate students from universities around the world. Linde Ostro and Scott Silver are Ph.D. candidates at Fordham University in New York who are completing a two-year study of the behavior of black howler monkeys in Belize's Cockscomb Basin Jaguar Reserve.

Studying animal behavior is a slow, difficult task in a tropical wilderness. Many of the howler monkeys have been fitted with radio collars, but it is still not easy to locate the troops when they are in the forest canopy one hundred feet above the ground. Also, the monkeys seldom range near the trails. So Linde and Scott must bushwhack through the forest with machetes, always keeping an eye out for the fer-de-lance and other venomous snakes.

Dear Megan,
Last night we went on a hike and I saw a red-eyed tree frog! A friend held it because he didn't have insect repellant on his hands. I did, and I didn't want to hurt the frog. I can't believe I really saw one in the wild!
Caitlin

Megan Johnson
28 South Street
Cin_____ Ohio
452__
U. __

*Holding a red-eyed tree frog*

# TREE FROGS AND THE GIANT MARINE TOAD

Tree frogs are named for where they live. They are able to move around their environment because of suction disks on their feet. They are small and are generally well camouflaged. However, some species are brightly colored, warning predators to stay away.

*Bufo marinus*, the giant marine toad, also lives in the rain forest. It is the largest toad in the world and has a peculiar adaptation to ward off predators. It secretes poisonous toxins onto its skin. Because it is so large, it is very tempting to predators. But an animal may die just from picking up one of these frogs in its mouth.

*A young marine toad*—Bufo marinus

# Dangerous Encounters in the Rain Forest

One night some hikers in the Cockscomb Basin Jaguar Preserve met a six-foot-long fer-de-lance, a really poisonous snake. It crossed the trail right behind them before they noticed it was there. Our Belizean guide, Nathan, said, "Do not disturb this

snake. If you get any closer it will definitely bite you."

The next night a different group found another poisonous snake, the coral snake. It is small, but very dangerous. These

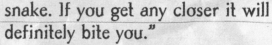

forests are filled with snakes, and several species are poisonous. In all, we spotted twelve venomous snakes in the forest, all at night.

Our leader, Stan, found another dangerous rain forest creature, a scorpion. We watched it by flashlight as it scurried around on the ground, but then it disappeared! That was a little scary!

Stan told us to see how many scorpions we could find. We thought he was joking,

A scorpion

but soon one kid spotted a few on the trunk of a thin tree. Then I saw three more. After a few minutes we realized it is dangerous to grab onto trees for support when hiking through the forest at night.

A tarantula

The next day Nathan found a tarantula's home. First, he poked a blade of grass down into the hole and then slowly pulled it out. The tarantula was holding onto the other end. Stan grabbed it by the abdomen and picked it up. It was about as big as the palm of my hand. With Nathan's help I touched it very carefully, then we let it go.

# Nathan Forbes

*For conservation efforts to work, there must be direct economic benefits for the local people. **Ecotourism** is one of the best ways for developing countries with pristine wilderness areas to generate income while at the same time protect their wild areas. But it has to be done well—with respect for the land and the people living on or near those wild areas.*

Nathan Forbes, a Belizean, is a naturalist and guide for International Expeditions, an ecotourism company. As part of his work as a naturalist, he identifies the region's plants and animals for visiting groups. He also teaches them about wildlife by catching insects, lizards, and even birds, allowing the groups to see them close-up and then releasing them quickly. Nathan also keeps the visitors safe in this exotic world. He points out the dangers of the tropics—the sting of the sea urchins or fire coral on the reef, the bite of venomous snakes and scorpions in the forest. Without Nathan, many travelers would learn the hard way.

*A boa constrictor covered with dewdrops in the early morning*

# FER-DE-LANCES, CORAL SNAKES, SCORPIONS, AND TARANTULAS

When visiting the rain forest, you have to watch out for and stay away from some creatures. The fer-de-lance is a tan snake with a dark brown diamond pattern. It can grow up to seven feet in length, and its bite can be lethal. Young ones can be particularly dangerous because their venom is more concentrated. It is a pit viper and has retractable fangs. These snakes live on the ground. The name comes from the triangular-shaped head and long body. They look like a lance or a spear.

*We saw this fer-de-lance while on an evening hike.*

Coral snakes are up to two feet long and have red, yellow, or black rings. Their bright colors may be a warning, for they are active both day

34

and night. Coral snakes can be found under rocks and logs, in many different habitats. They eat lizards and other snakes.

Not all snakes in the Neotropics are poisonous. There are many species of nonpoisonous snakes as well, including various harmless and beautiful vine snakes, the indigo snake, and the chunk-headed snake.

Scorpions sting rather than bite, and their sting is very painful—sometimes even deadly. The stinger is on the last segment of the scorpion's body, but it captures its prey with the claws at the front of its body. You have to be careful when you are staying in the rain forest to check your shoes and clothes for a hiding scorpion!

Tarantulas are poisonous, but not necessarily deadly to people. These spiders are nocturnal. If they rear up on their back legs it is a sign that they are threatened. Tarantulas walk with their front legs out as antennae. A tarantula's leg span can easily cover a person's hand.

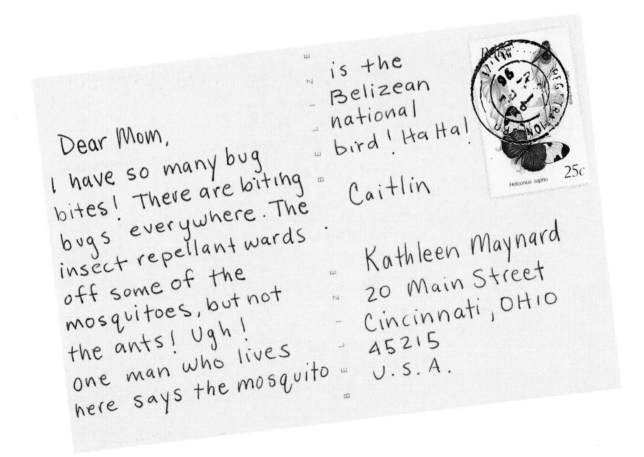

Dear Mom,
I have so many bug bites! There are biting bugs everywhere. The insect repellant wards off some of the mosquitoes, but not the ants! Ugh! One man who lives here says the mosquito is the Belizean national bird! Ha Ha!

Caitlin

Kathleen Maynard
20 Main Street
Cincinnati, OHIO
45215
U.S.A.

> ONE IMPORTANT NOTE ABOUT BIODIVERSITY—
> IF YOU WERE ABLE TO WEIGH ALL THE
> CREATURES IN A RAIN FOREST,
> over 90 percent would be insects and about
> one-third would be ants and termites!

## Mosquitoes and Botflies

The warm, moist tropics are great breeding grounds for mosquitoes. They are often called the most dangerous animal in the world because they may carry malaria, yellow fever, and other diseases. But, you can take medicine to protect yourself from these diseases and avoid most of the problems. And if you wear enough insect repellent, then the mosquitoes are just a nuisance. OK, a BIG nuisance.

However, the botfly is another story. I had a personal experience with this particular insect, and although it is interesting in terms of its life cycle, it is a real pain as well!

We came back from Belize with insect bites all over our bodies. The bites eventually faded away except for one on my leg that kept growing. My doctor said that it was an infected bug bite, and gave me an antibiotic. One day my Mom was putting a hot compress on the bite and saw something move! Then we knew that a botfly larva was living in my leg. My Dad had heard that one way to get rid of this creature was to tape a piece of raw meat over it so it would burrow into the meat. We tried this but it didn't work. My doctor had to cut it out.

How did it get in my leg? In Belize, a botfly egg was transferred to my leg from a mosquito when it bit me. The eggs survive only by hatching into a host animal—me. The animal feeds on the host until it is large enough to emerge. And how does the egg of the botfly get onto the mosquito? Amazingly, the female botfly captures a female mosquito in flight and lays an egg on the mosquito's beak. When the mosquito bit me, the egg stayed in my leg, eventually growing large enough for us to see. Now, besides all my wonderful memories of my rain forest trip, I also have a souvenir scar.

*Insect nests*

Jan Meerman, an entomologist who studies butterflies and moths, with a Sphingid moth on his pocket

# Jan Meerman

Entomologists are biologists who study some of the world's smallest and most numerous creatures—insects. And in a tropical forest, there are far more insects than everything else combined. Dr. Jan Meerman is a Dutch entomologist who has lived in the tropics for many years, and discovered a number of "new" insect species that were unknown to science. He has also identified some species of moth that were not previously known to live in Belize.

Jan and his wife live in a small wooden house in the forest and he cheerfully describes the annual invasion of the army ant, a species that moves through the forest like a river, swallowing up all other insects in its path. Once a year the Meermans perch on stools and watch millions of army ants pour over the wall into their house, march across their bed, through the kitchen, and out the other end of the house. On their way through, the army ants round up and eat every roach and scorpion in the house, serving as nature's pest control.

*Army ants*

We left the rain forest to begin our reef studies, but we found we were not quite finished with "trees." Out first snorkeling experience was in the mangroves, the beneficial plants that line coastal areas.

Mangroves is a general name for coastal plants that tolerate seawater. There are quite a few different mangrove species, all of which are an important part of Neotropical coastal **ecosystems.** Mangroves grow along the coastline, the edges of cayes (islands), and lagoons. If not constantly submerged in water, they are flooded off and on throughout the year. The leaves of mangroves are coated with wax that keeps their precious moisture from evaporating. Their clumsy looking prop roots take hold in the soft sands of tidal zones and hold them steady through tropical storms.

Mangroves help protect the coast from hurricane damage, and they rebound quickly after the storms. Mangroves also keep fishes' eggs safe from currents and waves. Therefore, many fish begin their lives in the mangrove ecosystem. Many birds and other animals live and are sheltered in the mangroves, too.

*Sea life amid the mangrove roots*

It was exciting to finally be in the water, snorkeling in the mangroves. We saw dozens of different types of fish. We didn't use flippers because the sediment that the plants use for soil is easily stirred up. If that happens, the water gets really murky, and we wouldn't be able to see very much of the diversity in the mangroves.

Diving among the shallow roots of the mangrove trees gave us a wonderful introduction to coastal ecosystems. The mangroves are home to many kinds of life. Colonies of magnificent frigate birds, or "man-'o-war birds," were roosting on the roots and branches of the trees and spiraling up in search of food. They have a seven-foot wingspan, with sharply pointed wings like other ocean-soaring birds. They glide above the blue water looking for fish.

*Magnificent frigate bird*

The "magnificent" in their name refers to the male's scarlet throat sac which the bird inflates to attract a mate. The name "man-'o-war bird" is derived from the bird's habit of robbing gulls, pelicans, and other birds of their catches.

At first, the mangroves did not seem so amazing. But once you are in the water, peering through the submerged roots, you begin to notice the tens of thousands of small fish. By trapping sediment and nutrients, the mangroves serve as "nurseries," or feeding stations, for thousands of fish species that are important to commercial fisheries and recreational divers. Mangrove trees grow quickly, and as their leaves and branches fall into the surrounding water, they serve as food for everything from micro-organisms to juvenile fish, thus playing a huge role in the food web of the cayes and the coral reefs.

The coast of the state of Florida and the Florida Keys were once lined with mangrove forests. While it is easy to clear the mangroves, it is not so easy to regrow them. Coastal development must be curtailed if mangroves are to be protected.

*Schools of small fish swimming through the mangrove roots*

## Coral Reefs are Cool

Imagine how thrilled eighteen midwestern American teenagers were to spend a week at the beach. After being eaten alive by the bugs in the heat and humidity of the rain forest, we thought we were in heaven. We put on our swimsuits, tons of

*Snorkeling in the coral reef*

sunscreen, grabbed our snorkeling gear, and hit the reef. After our first few hours we came out of the water excited and full of questions. What are the names of all those hundreds of fish, coral, and other invertebrates? We wanted to identify them, but we also were curious about how everything fit together. What were the interrelationships in this abundant ecosystem? How do the pieces of this colorful mosaic fit together?

## BIOFACTS

**A TROPICAL CORAL REEF CAN SUPPORT UP TO THREE THOUSAND SPECIES OF FISH AND INVERTEBRATES.**

Unfortunately, poachers steal fifteen hundred tons of coral to make into the trinkets you see sold on the streets and in airport shops.

## STARTING SHALLOW

Most of the group had been to the ocean before, but there is a big difference between wading at the beach and swimming for hours at a time out over our heads in unfamiliar waters. Before this trip we had a training session with some dive instructors to learn the basics of snorkeling—basics like spreading toothpaste on the inside of your mask to keep it from fogging up, how to clear your snorkel instead of swallowing salt water, and how to clear your ears as you swim down so they don't hurt from the water pressure.

*Ranguana Caye on the Belizean barrier reef—a wonderful spot for snorkeling*

Fortunately, it's easier to swim in the ocean than in a pool. Salt water makes things buoyant, so you don't have to tread water. You can simply float on the surface and explore the reef with your eyes, moving slowly with just a small kick of your flippers.

Our first lesson on the reef was about what *not* to touch. Sea urchins have sharp spines that pack a painful sting and should be avoided. Fire coral is so dangerous that you need to stay far away. The razorlike edges carry a venom that can permanently scar a diver, ruin a good day's diving, or sometimes even land you in the hospital.

# THE COLORS OF THE REEF

The colors of the reef are brightest and best seen in the light toward the water's surface. For close inspection of fish, coral, and other reef creatures, our best dives were in areas twelve to fifteen feet deep. We floated above the reef and then dove down to inspect or even try to lure a fish or lobster out of its hole. During one dive we swam between branches of a giant elkhorn coral. It was like flying through tree branches in a forest. The fish just ignored us and let us swim among them.

*Elkhorn coral*

45

The most colorful of the fish were the reef fish swimming and hiding in the coral itself: yellows and blues on angelfish, purple and orange on the fairy basslet, dramatic stripes on the moray eels. But my favorites were the faster open-water fish cruising along the reef in search of dinner. Schools of leery bonefish bolted past us. They were so fast they seemed to swim right through us, though not one fin touched our skin. The shiny silver barracuda caused other fish to hide. It was easy to hook, but hard to land on a flyrod. And then there were the sharks. Yes, we swam with sharks, but it wasn't as scary as I had imagined.

## JUST OVER THE EDGE

Our last day of diving was out over the edge of the reef, where the sea bottom falls off like the edge of a shelf. Because we were far from shore, we dove from our boats. It was a calm day, with gentle two-foot swells,

*A boat took us out to an island at the edge of the reef for deepwater diving.*

but a lot of us felt pretty seasick once the boats' motors were turned off and we just bobbed up and down. We'd been told that it wasn't nearly so bad in the water, and once we dove in and started snorkeling everything was fine.

Here we were diving in deep water. Some of our guides swam down thirty-five feet and sat on the bottom looking at fish. One boy in our group tried that but swam right back up. The fish were much bigger in the open

*Deepwater fish*

water. We saw six- to seven-foot-long stingrays "flying" slowly with a flap of their winglike fins.

The first shark we saw was a nurse shark. We knew this isn't a "man-eater," but we kept our distance. Our leader, Stan, swam down near it, but the shark just went on its way. We also saw a lemon shark, which was far enough away so that it didn't make me nervous—or maybe just a little bit nervous. In all there are 325 different species of sharks. Some are huge, like the 40-foot-long, 13-ton whale shark. Others are as small as your hand, like the dogfish. Only about a dozen shark species are known to attack people and most shark attacks happen in the Indian and Pacific Oceans. In the Caribbean Sea on the coast of Belize, there have been very few shark attacks over the years. The tiger sharks and lemon sharks are the ones to watch out for. Believe it or not, most other sharks are more afraid of you than you are of them.

*A nurse shark*

# ANATOMY OF A CORAL REEF

A coral reef is made up of millions of tiny corals. Corals are animals that belong to the phylum that includes sea jellies and sea anemones, but they are smaller. Each coral is a tiny polyp with a calcium carbonate skeleton. When millions of corals cluster together, they build up a large reef. The living coral is on the top layer, resting on the structure built up over tens of thousands of previous generations.

*A coral reef*

There's more to a reef ecosystem than the coral itself. Like the rain forest, a coral reef is a community of living things. Not many animals eat the coral, but they do eat each other. Reefs need clear water to survive because tiny algae-like organisms, zooxanthellae, live in the tissue of the coral polyps and need sunlight to grow. So water muddied by runoff from erosion or other disturbances can kill a reef.

The coral is a fairly simple animal. Its hollow, tubelike body has a single opening at the top which serves as its mouth. The mouth is ringed by stinging tentacles, but their venom is generally not strong enough to hurt divers.

Coral

A coral polyp

Scientists have discovered about 5,000 species of coral, 60 of which are found in the Caribbean Sea. Not all the coral species are reef builders. Coral reefs occur in tropical areas between 20 degrees North latitude and 20 degrees South latitude. The barrier reef along the coast of Belize, Honduras, and southern Mexico is one of the largest and most beautiful in the world. In length, it is second only to the Great Barrier Reef off eastern Australia.

Coral reefs are one of the most diverse ecosystems on Earth. With so much coral diversity, there are naturally different types of reefs. *Fringe reefs* build up on coastal areas or on the edges of cayes. *Atolls* are built of rings of coral that once fringed an island that eventually sank, leaving the coral behind. *Barrier reefs* are off shore and run parallel to the coast.

Over time, coral reefs build up the land. The Florida Keys, for example, were created from ancient coral reefs. The reef-building is accomplished by the hard corals, but there are also soft corals, such as sea fans and sea whips, that secrete a soft, flexible skeleton. The way to tell soft and hard coral apart is to inspect their polyps—the individual coral animals. Soft coral have eight feathery tentacles on each polyp. Hard coral polyps may have from six tentacles to dozens, but never eight.

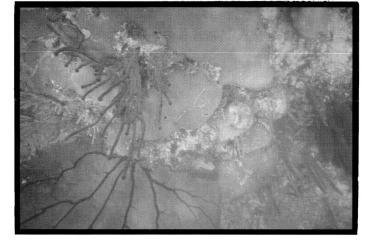

Coral sea fans

# TROPICAL TERMINOLOGY

## WHAT IS ECOLOGY ANYWAY?

Ecology is the study of the interrelationships among living things and nonliving things, within a community of plants and animals. An ecosystem includes things you might expect, like predator-prey relationships in a given area, and some you might not, like the water and nutrient flow through the area.

## DANGEROUS ENCOUNTERS ON THE REEF

### NURSE SHARK

A nurse shark has two whiskerlike barbels hanging from its upper lip. It also has two dorsal fins of nearly equal size and lacks the lower lobe on the tail fin. This shark is a fairly common one. Nurse sharks have small mouths on the bottom of their snouts. They feed on **invertebrates** from the ocean floor and are known to bite humans only when provoked.

### STINGRAY

The stingray is a bottom-dwelling cousin of the shark. All rays have large pectoral fins that they flap, somewhat like a bird moves its wings, as they travel through the water. Stingrays get their name from the sharp,

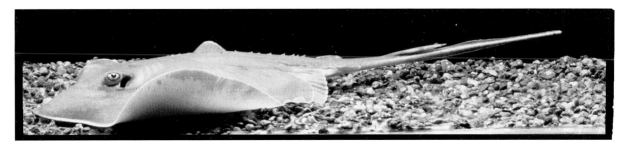

*A stingray*

venomous spines on their tails. Stingrays are common in the sandy areas near the reefs, but may go unnoticed since they often lie completely still, partially covered with sand.

## SCORPION FISH

The spotted scorpion fish is the most common scorpion fish on Neotropical reefs. The name comes from the deadly venom that is their best defense against predation. You are most likely to find a scorpion fish lying motionless on the reef, blending almost perfectly into its background.

*A scorpion fish*

## SEA URCHINS

Sea urchins are amazing creatures that divers and waders should avoid touching. They are members of the phylum Echinodermata, which gets its name from the ancient Greek words *"echinos"* and *"derma"* meaning "hedgehog-like skin." Although echinoderms also include sea stars and sea cucumbers, the name certainly fits sea urchins. The sea urchin has foot-long spines. They carry little venom; the pain is caused by the spine itself, the tip of which is barbed and remains under your skin. So rubbing it makes it worse.

## SEASTARS

Neither a star nor a fish, the so-called "starfish" is actually an echino-derm. Typically benthic, or bottom dwelling, sea stars come in a wide variety of colors and sizes, with most having five arms. All sea stars are predators, some species feed on animals as small as floating zoo-plankton, while others pre-fer worms, crustaceans, and even oysters.

To digest an oyster, the sea star pulls open the two shells, holding on tightly with its tube feet. Once a small crack is available, the sea star sticks its stomach out through its own mouth, allows its digestive juices to dissolve the oyster, and then squishes its stomach back into its body for complete digestion!

*A seastar*

## MORAY EELS

Moray eels look frightening, but unless provoked, they are harmless to humans. Their teeth are sharp, but not venomous. They continuously open and close their mouths, as if about to bite, and look scary. However, moray eels do this to force water over their gills in order to breathe. The green moray is actually a blue-gray fish completely covered with yellowish mucus. They often hide in holes and crevices in the coral, so only a foot or so of their six-foot bodies protrudes from the reef.

*A moray eel*

## SAVING RAIN FORESTS AND REEFS

Protecting biodiversity and saving wild areas is in our own best interest. So get the word out about how important it is to save wild habitats and encourage your friends and family to get involved. Saving rain forests isn't just about saving jaguars, boa constrictors, and parrots. It's really about saving ourselves. The same thing is true for the coral reefs. In addition to being beautiful and tranquil places for us to visit and explore, coral reefs are essential for the economic well-being of the tropical nations where they occur. Countries like Belize, Jamaica, and Australia, to name a few, need healthy reefs to have a prosperous fishing industry. Look at the coastal region of Haiti, where the reefs are silted over by erosion from clear-cutting on the land, and you will see how overuse can destroy an area.

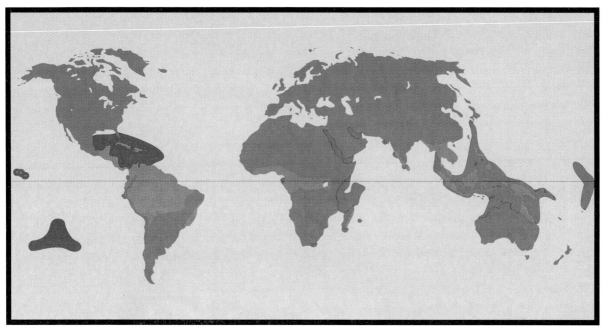

■ *Tropical Rain Forests* ■ *Coral Reefs*

The destruction of the tropical rain forests and reefs is a huge problem. Many things need to be done to turn this mess around. Since only a mammoth solution will work, we put together "The Elephant's Solution" to sum up what it will take to protect nature.

## ENVIRONMENTAL EDUCATION

Teaching all people, from New York City to the villages of the Amazon, to care about wildlife and wild places is the key to the preservation of the world.

## LAWS PROTECTING WILDLIFE

Enforcing legislation saves habitats and stops the illegal poaching and trade in wildlife.

## ECOSYSTEM AND SPECIES LEVEL RESEARCH

Exploring entire living ecosystems helps scientists understand what needs to be done to protect biodiversity.

*A margay*

## POPULATION PLANNING

In 1830 the world's human population was one billion—today it's nearly six billion. Planning for the future means planning now!

## HABITAT PROTECTION

Protecting as much of the Earth's remaining wild places as possible is the key to protecting nature's astounding biodiversity. Today less than 5 percent of the Earth's land areas are in national parks and protected areas.

## ALTERNATIVE INCOME
## FOR LOCAL PEOPLE

Developing sustainable, community-based programs to provide alternative income for local people reduces pressures on natural areas. This is true in Yellowstone National Park as well as in the rain forests of the tropics.

## NATIVE SPECIES,
## NOT INTRODUCED ONES

Prevent the introduction of non-native species of plants and animals, and take steps to remove introduced ones.

## TECHNICAL TRAINING
## IN CONSERVATION

Providing technical training for local people ensures the protection of national parks and reserves.

## SUSTAINABLE USE OF
## WILD PLACES AND SPECIES

Develop ways to create a balance between people and wildlife.

*An emerald toucanet*

Conservation groups and determined individuals are working hard to protect the remaining wilderness in Belize. The Belize Audubon Society works with conservation issues and has encouraged the enjoyment, not exploitation, of nature. The Belize Zoo and Tropical Education Center is

*A Baird's tapir at the Belize Zoo*

dedicated to demonstrating the importance of saving wild areas and wild animals for the people of Belize. It is the best place to take your camera because you can get much closer to the hawks, jaguars, tapirs, and crocodiles than in the forests and swamps.

# Tony Garel

When the Belize Zoo was founded in 1983 Tony Garel was a teenager, and one of its first employees. Starting as a bird keeper, he is now the general curator and is responsible for the entire zoo collection. Today the Belize Zoo and Tropical Education Center is run by and for Belizeans. The new name reflects its commitment to educating everyone living in this Central American nation about their rich wildlife heritage and the importance of protecting it for future generations.

In addition to managing the zookeepers and monitoring the health, breeding, and nutrition of the animals, Tony represents the organization throughout Belize and around the world. He is the author of a book on the reptiles of Belize and appears regularly on nationwide television broadcasts. Tony has also traveled throughout North America and Europe to work with other zoos on wildlife husbandry and conservation, and to spread the word of the conservation success of the Belize Zoo and Tropical Education Center.

There are many ways to help protect rain forests and reefs. You can join with others to learn more and help get the word out. Or you can use your skills to write about or raise money to help preserve wild areas. Figure out how you can get involved. A good system for finding out what you can do is what environmentalists call the three "I"s:

Get INFORMED
Find out the facts by visiting the library and talking with experts.

Get INVOLVED
Once you know what needs to be done, don't hide it. Share it, explain it, talk about it.

Get IN FOCUS
Choose an area of interest or involvement and stick to it. Become your town's expert on an issue and you'll be able to get others involved, too.

HOW DO I GET THERE?

International Expeditions
1 Environs Park
Helena, AL 35080

Island Institute Whale &
Marine Biology Camp
P.O. Box 661
Vashon Island, WA 98070

JASON Foundation
for Education
395 Totten Pond Road
Waltham, MA 02154

NOLS
288 Main Street
Lander, WY 82520

Organization For Tropical Studies
Geostar Travel, Inc.
1240 Century Court
Santa Rosa, CA 95403

Sea Camp
Newfound Harbor Marine Institute
Route 3, Box 170
Big Pine Key, FL 33043

Check out the tropical travel programs offered by local nature centers, zoos, natural history museums, or aquariums.

## WHO'S DOING WHAT?

These organizations work to get kids directly involved in protecting wildlife and wild places. Send them postcards asking how you can help.

Adopt-an-Acre
The Nature Conservancy
1815 N. Lynn Street
Arlington, VA 22209

Belize Zoo and
Tropical Education Center
Box 1787
Belize City
Belize, Central America

Earth Force
1501 Wilson Boulevard
Arlington, VA 22209

Ecosystem Survival Plan
1 Zoo Road
San Francisco, CA 94132

Kids F.A.C.E.
Box 158254
Nashville, TN 37215

Kids for Saving Earth
Box 47247
Plymouth, MN 55447

Save the Rain Forest
604 Jamie Street
Dodgeville, WI 53533

YMCA Earth Service Corps
Metro YMCA
909 4th Avenue
Seattle, WA 98104

**Biodiversity**—the natural variation of species that provides the genetic base for all life on earth.

**Canopy**—the crowns, or tops, of tropical rain forest trees that form a dense leafy layer shading the forest floor.

**Ecosystem**—interrelating plants, animals, and microorganisms and their environment.

**Ecotourism**—travel programs that promote better understanding and involvement in natural areas.

**Ethnobotanist**—a scientist who studies the plant lore of a people.

**Fungus**—one of a group of plants that lacks leaves and green color and that feeds upon plant or animal matter. Molds and mushrooms are kind's of fungus.

**Habitat**—the place (area and physical conditions) where a plant or animal species is usually found in the wild.

**Invertebrates**—animals without vertebrae columns, or backbones.

**Lagoons**—a shallow pond, sound, or water channel near or connected with a larger body of water.

**Mangroves**—groups of tropical trees or shrubs that have adapted to a salty environment, and which form dense masses of roots at the edge of the sea.

**Mutualism**—a kind of symbiosis in which both organisms benefit.

**Neotropics**—the tropical regions of Central and South America.

**Primatologist**—a scientist who studies primates, the order of mammals that includes monkeys, apes, prosimians, and humans.

**Rain forest**—a humid evergreen forest found at low elevation in regions between the Tropics of Cancer and Capricorn. Tropical rain forests have abundant rainfall and warm temperatures all year.

**Savanna**—a tropical or subtropical grassland with scattered trees and drought-resistant undergrowth.

**Symbiosis**—the living together of two different organisms in a relationship from which one or both benefit. See mutualism.

**Translocate**—The movement, by humans, of wild animals or plants from one area to another.

**Tropics**—the regions of the Earth on each side of and parallel to the equator.

**Vertebrates**—animals with backbones.

Forsyth, Adrian. *Journey Through a Tropical Jungle.* New York: Simon and Schuster, 1989.

Halpern, Robert R. *Green Planet Rescue: Saving the Earth's Endangered Plants.* New York: Franklin Watts, 1993.

Jenike, David, and Mark Jenike. *A Walk Through a Rain Forest: Life in the Ituri Forest of Zaire.* New York: Franklin Watts, 1994.

Johnson, Rebecca L. *The Great Barrier Reef: A Living Laboratory.* Minneapolis: Lerner, 1991.

Lampton, Christopher. *Coral Reefs in Danger.* Brookfield, CT: Millbrook, 1992.

Landau, Elaine. *Tropical Rain Forests around the World.* New York: Franklin Watts, 1992.

Mallory, Kenneth. *Waterhole: Life in a Rescued Tropical Forest.* New York: Franklin Watts, 1992.

Miller, Christina. *Jungle Rescue: Saving the New World Tropical Rain Forests.* New York: Atheneum, 1991.

Sargent, William. *Night Reef: Dusk to Dawn on a Coral Reef.* New York: Franklin Watts, 1991.

Tayntor, Elizabeth, Paul Erickson, and Les Kaufman. *Dive to the Coral Reefs.* New York: Crown, 1986.